THE LIFE OF DOLORES HUERTA

BY GILLIA M. OLSON

SEQUENCE

AMICUS | AMICUS INK

Sequence is published by Amicus and Amicus Ink
P.O. Box 227, Mankato, MN 56002
www.amicuspublishing.us

Library of Congress Cataloging-in-Publication Data
Names: Olson, Gillia M., author.
Title: The life of Dolores Huerta / by Gillia M. Olson.
Description: Mankato, MN : Amicus, [2022] | Series: Sequence | Series: Change maker biographies | Includes bibliographical references and index. | Audience: Ages 7–10 | Audience: Grades 2–3
Identifiers: LCCN 2019036114 (print) | LCCN 2019036115 (ebook) | ISBN 9781645490333 (PDF) | ISBN 9781681525952 (Paperback) | ISBN 9781681519487 (Library Binding)
Subjects: LCSH: Huerta, Dolores, 1930- | Women labor leaders–United States–Biography–Juvenile literature. | Mexican American women labor union members–Biography–Juvenile literature. | Mexican American migrant agricultural laborers–Labor unions–Organizing–History–Juvenile literature. | Human rights workers–United States–Biography–Juvenile literature. | Social justice–United States–Juvenile literature.
Classification: LCC HD6509.H84 (ebook) | LCC HD6509.H84 O57 2022 (print) | DDC 331.4/7813092 [B] -- dc23
LC record available at https://lccn.loc.gov/2019036114

Editor: Alissa Thielges
Designer: Ciara Beitlich
Photo Researcher: Marty Levick

Photo Credits: Shutterstock/Richard Thornton cover; Wikimedia/Jay Godwin cover; Alamy/Jason Mendez/Everett Collection/Alamy Live News 5; The Haggin Museum, Stockton, California 6–7; Library of Congress/Dorothea Lange 9; Getty/Cathy Murphy 10, 23; Stanford University Library/Bob Fitch 12–13; AP/Walter Zeboski 14–15; Getty/Arthur Schatz 17; Walter Reuther Library 18, 20–21; AP/Merced Sun-Star, Marci Stenberg 24–25; AP/Carolyn Kaster 27; Shutterstock/Music4mix 28

TABLE OF CONTENTS

Yes, She Can!

Dolores Huerta knows people have the power to make a change. She's seen it in action. She came up with the saying, "*¡Sí, se puede!*" It is Spanish for, "Yes, we can!" At the time, she was a young **Hispanic** woman fighting for workers' rights. She's fought for women's rights, the environment, and human rights.

LOADING . . . LOADING . . . LOADING . . .

Dolores never gives up. She still fights for equal rights today.

LOADING . . . LOADING . . . LOADING . . .

Dolores is born in Dawson, New Mexico.

APRIL 10, 1930

LOADING . . . LOADING . . .

Dolores Huerta was born April 10, 1930, in New Mexico. At age three, she moved with her mother to Stockton, California. Her grandfather often took care of Dolores and her siblings. Dolores talked a lot. Her grandfather called her "Seven Tongues." Her mother worked hard. She later bought a hotel and restaurant. Her mother's hard work inspired Dolores.

A 1930 photo shows the busy Main Street in Stockton.

LOADING . . . LOADING . . . LOADING . . .

Dolores finished high school in 1948. She went to college. She became a teacher. Many of her students were children of farm workers. They came to school hungry and dirty. Some had no shoes. Families lived in shacks with dirt floors. Parents worked all day with no breaks. They made less than $1 an hour.

Farm workers made very little money. Some lived in camps near the fields.

Dolores is born in Dawson, New Mexico.

APRIL 10, 1930

1948

Dolores graduates high school in Stockton, California.

DING . . . LOADING . . .

LOADING... LOADING... LOADING...

Dolores stands with Fred Ross. Together they improved life for farm workers.

- APRIL 10, 1930 — Dolores is born in Dawson, New Mexico.
- 1948 — Dolores graduates high school in Stockton, California.
- 1955 — Dolores helps start the Stockton chapter of CSO.

. . . LOADING . . .

Strikes, Boycotts, and Protests

Dolores thought she could help these families. She quit teaching. In 1955, she and Fred Ross started the Community Service Organization (CSO). The group worked for rights for Mexican Americans. She **lobbied** the state government. She talked to lawmakers. Her efforts helped. New laws were passed. Voting and driving tests were now available in Spanish.

LOADING . . . LOADING . . . LOADING . . .

Dolores wanted to do more. At the time, farm workers could not form **unions** like other workers. That didn't stop Dolores. In 1962, she and Cesar Chavez started the National Farm Workers Association (NFWA). It wasn't an official union yet. But the group worked for farm workers' rights. It pushed for aid for **migrant** farm workers and their families. The NFWA later merged with another group. It became the United Farm Workers (UFW).

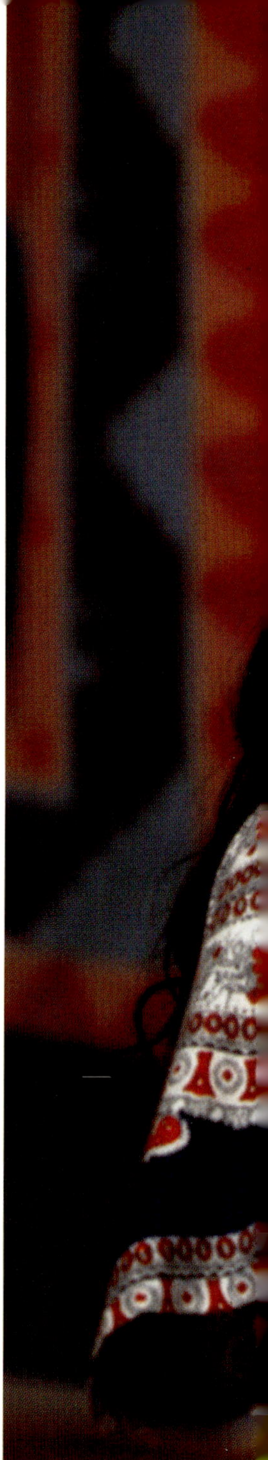

APRIL 10, 1930 — Dolores is born in Dawson, New Mexico.

1948 — Dolores graduates high school in Stockton, California.

1955 — Dolores helps start the Stockton chapter of CSO.

1962 — Dolores and Cesar Chavez form the National Farm Workers Association.

ADING . . .

Dolores and Cesar Chavez speak at the first United Farm Workers meeting.

LOADING . . . LOADING . . . LOADING . . .

Grape pickers hold signs to announce that they are on **strike**. "Huelga" means strike in Spanish.

- APRIL 10, 1930 — Dolores is born in Dawson, New Mexico.
- 1948 — Dolores graduates high school in Stockton, California.
- 1955 — Dolores helps start the Stockton chapter of CSO.
- 1962 — Dolores and Cesar Chavez form the National Farm Workers Association.
- 1965 — Dolores helps lead the Delano grape strike and boycott.

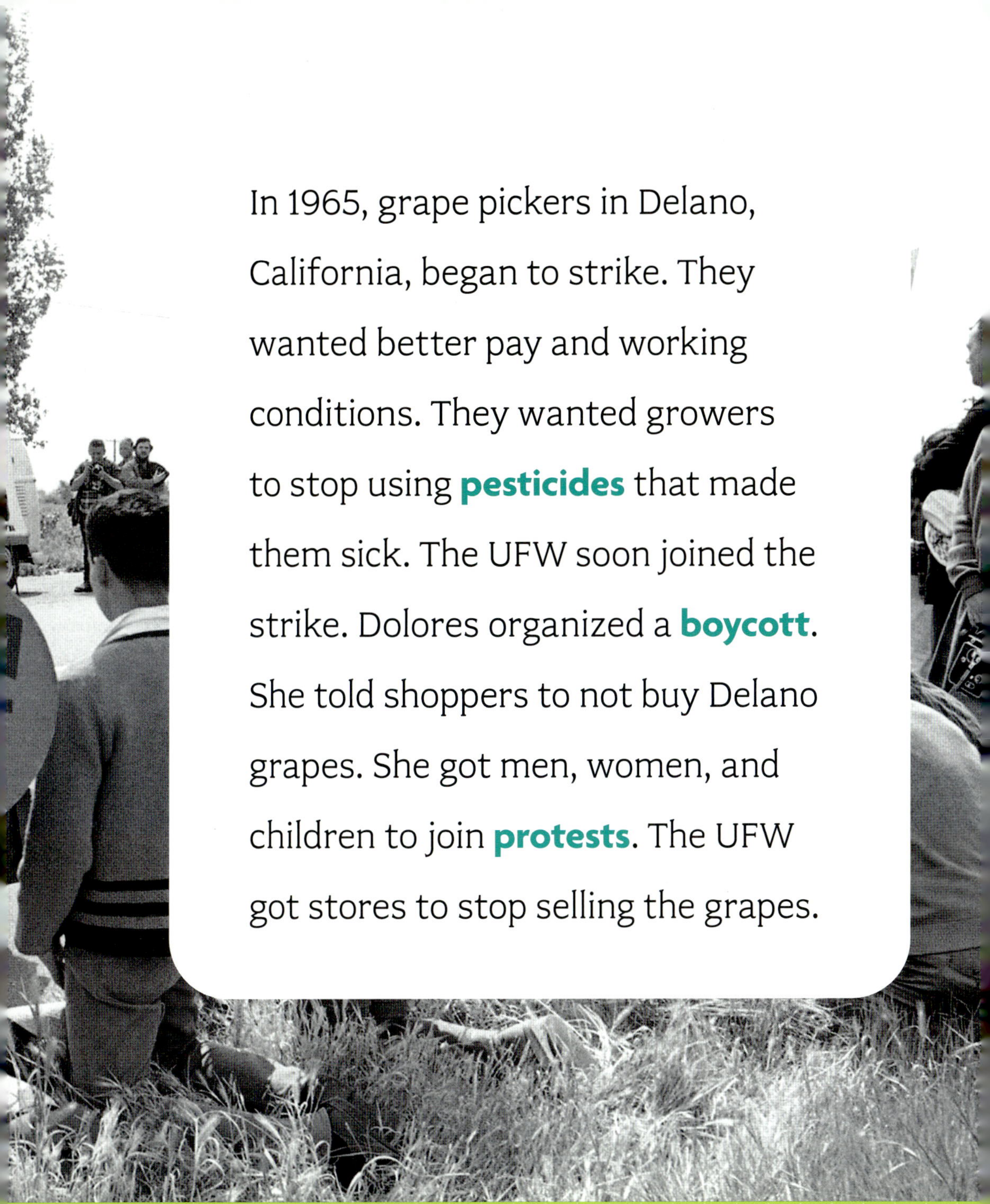

In 1965, grape pickers in Delano, California, began to strike. They wanted better pay and working conditions. They wanted growers to stop using **pesticides** that made them sick. The UFW soon joined the strike. Dolores organized a **boycott**. She told shoppers to not buy Delano grapes. She got men, women, and children to join **protests**. The UFW got stores to stop selling the grapes.

LOADING . . . LOADING . . . LOADING . . .

The boycott ended in 1970. Their demands were met: better pay and no pesticides while they worked.

Dolores's phrase, "*¡Sí, se puede!*" inspired all farm workers. By 1975, her work led to the California Agricultural Labor Relations Act. Farm worker unions were now accepted by the government. The UFW could legally enforce good working conditions and better pay.

Dolores works as the UFW vice president during the boycott.

- **April 10, 1930:** Dolores is born in Dawson, New Mexico.
- **1948:** Dolores graduates high school in Stockton, California.
- **1955:** Dolores helps start the Stockton chapter of CSO.
- **1962:** Dolores and Cesar Chavez form the National Farm Workers Association.
- **1965:** Dolores helps lead the Delano grape strike and boycott.
- **1975:** The California Agricultural Labor Relations Act is passed.

LOADING . . . LOADING . . . LOADING . . .

Dolores (center) stands with members of the UFW around 1980.

APRIL 10, 1930	1948	1955	1962	1965	1975
Dolores is born in Dawson, New Mexico.	Dolores graduates high school in Stockton, California.	Dolores helps start the Stockton chapter of CSO.	Dolores and Cesar Chavez form the National Farm Workers Association.	Dolores helps lead the Delano grape strike and boycott.	The California Agricultural Labor Relations Act is passed.

A Tireless Worker

Dolores worked for the UFW into the 1980s. She kept fighting against pesticides. She spoke to lawmakers. She joined protests.

In 1986, Dolores pushed for an **immigration** law. It passed. It let migrants work in the United States legally. It also let those already living here stay legally.

Dolores successfully lobbies for the Immigration Reform and Control Act.

1986

. . LOADING . . . LOADING . . .

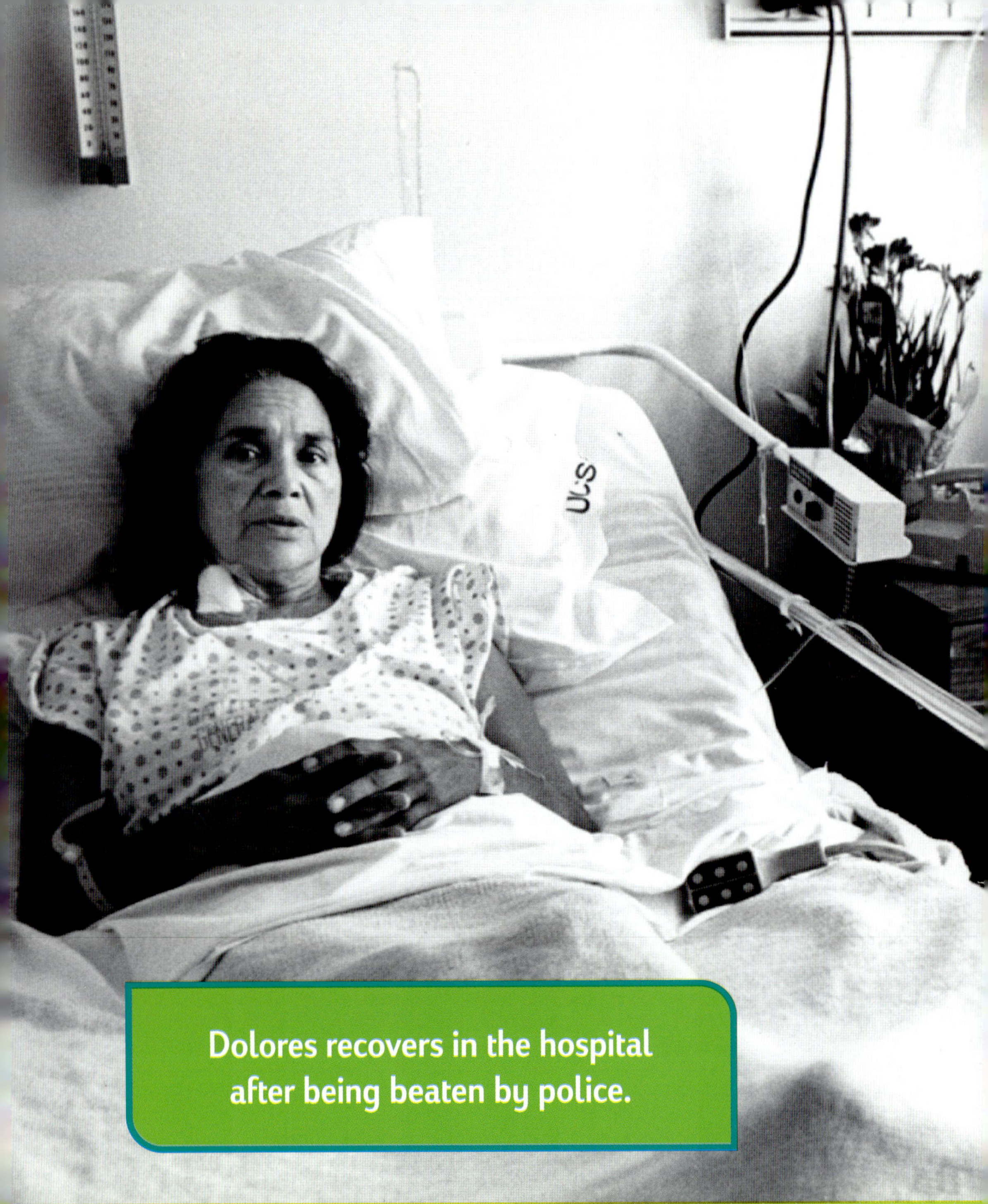

Dolores recovers in the hospital after being beaten by police.

APRIL 10, 1930	1948	1955	1962	1965	1975
Dolores is born in Dawson, New Mexico.	Dolores graduates high school in Stockton, California.	Dolores helps start the Stockton chapter of CSO.	Dolores and Cesar Chavez form the National Farm Workers Association.	Dolores helps lead the Delano grape strike and boycott.	The California Agricultural Labor Relations Act is passed.

Dolores often faced violence during protests. Guns were pointed at her. People tried to run her over. She was arrested 22 times. In September of 1988, Dolores was in a protest in San Francisco. She was badly beaten by a police officer. She sued and won. As a result, San Francisco changed how their police control crowds.

Dolores successfully lobbies for the Immigration Reform and Control Act.

1986

1988

DING . . . LOADING . . .

Dolores is badly beaten by a police officer during a peaceful protest.

More Than Labor Rights

While Dolores healed, she spent time with her 11 children. She had seven children from two marriages. She also had four children with Robert Chavez, Cesar's brother.

As she got better, she worked for women's rights. Dolores worked with Feminist Majority in 1992. She helped women get elected as lawmakers.

- **APRIL 10, 1930** — Dolores is born in Dawson, New Mexico.
- **1948** — Dolores graduates high school in Stockton, California.
- **1955** — Dolores helps start the Stockton chapter of CSO.
- **1962** — Dolores and Cesar Chavez form the National Farm Workers Association.
- **1965** — Dolores helps lead the Delano grape strike and boycott.
- **1975** — The California Agricultural Labor Relations Act is passed.

Dolores sits with two of her young daughters around the mid-1970s.

Dolores successfully lobbies for the Immigration Reform and Control Act.

Dolores works with Feminist Majority.

1986

1988

1992

...LOADING...

Dolores is badly beaten by a police officer during a peaceful protest.

APRIL 10, 1930: Dolores is born in Dawson, New Mexico.

1948: Dolores graduates high school in Stockton, California.

1955: Dolores helps start the Stockton chapter of CSO.

1962: Dolores and Cesar Chavez form the National Farm Workers Association.

1965: Dolores helps lead the Delano grape strike and boycott.

1975: The California Agricultural Labor Relations Act is passed.

Dolores continued to work for the UFW and women's rights. She also wanted to help people make changes in their own towns. In 2002, she started the Dolores Huerta Foundation. It teaches people how to organize for a cause. It helps them become leaders in their communities.

In 2002, Dolores led a 150-mile march to Sacramento, California. The UFW wanted the governor to sign a farm labor bill.

1986 — Dolores successfully lobbies for the Immigration Reform and Control Act.

1988 — Dolores is badly beaten by a police officer during a peaceful protest.

1992 — Dolores works with Feminist Majority.

2002 — Dolores starts the Dolores Huerta Foundation.

OADING . . .

Continuing to Inspire

Dolores has received many awards for her work. In 2012, she received the highest honor from the president. Barack Obama gave her the Presidential Medal of Freedom. Dolores was happy her work was respected. Her goal is to help others make a change. She knows people can make a difference.

President Obama places the Medal of Freedom around Dolores' neck.

APRIL 10, 1930	Dolores is born in Dawson, New Mexico.
1948	Dolores graduates high school in Stockton, California.
1955	Dolores helps start the Stockton chapter of CSO.
1962	Dolores and Cesar Chavez form the National Farm Workers Association.
1965	Dolores helps lead the Delano grape strike and boycott.
1975	The California Agricultural Labor Relations Act is passed.

- 1986 — Dolores successfully lobbies for the Immigration Reform and Control Act.
- 1988 — Dolores is badly beaten by a police officer during a peaceful protest.
- 1992 — Dolores works with Feminist Majority.
- 2002 — Dolores starts the Dolores Huerta Foundation.
- 2012 — Dolores receives the Presidential Medal of Freedom.

- **April 10, 1930**: Dolores is born in Dawson, New Mexico.
- **1948**: Dolores graduates high school in Stockton, California.
- **1955**: Dolores helps start the Stockton chapter of CSO.
- **1962**: Dolores and Cesar Chavez form the National Farm Workers Association.
- **1965**: Dolores helps lead the Delano grape strike and boycott.
- **1975**: The California Agricultural Labor Relations Act is passed.

Dolores still speaks all over the country. She supports equal rights for all. Her foundation held Bakersfield's first gay pride parade in 2018. That year, California declared her birthday as Dolores Huerta Day. She inspires people to make their town, and the world, a better place.

Dolores rides in a parade to celebrate Mexican Independence Day.

- **1986** Dolores successfully lobbies for the Immigration Reform and Control Act.
- **1988** Dolores is badly beaten by a police officer during a peaceful protest.
- **1992** Dolores works with Feminist Majority.
- **2002** Dolores starts the Dolores Huerta Foundation.
- **2012** Dolores receives the Presidential Medal of Freedom.
- **2018** California declares April 10 as Dolores Huerta Day.

Glossary

boycott To join with others to refuse to buy from someone to force them to meet demands.

Hispanic A person living in the United States who is from, or their family is from, a Spanish-speaking country.

immigration Travel into a foreign country to live.

lobby To try to convince lawmakers to pass certain laws.

migrant A person who moves regularly to find work.

pesticide A chemical used to destroy insects that damage crops or livestock; it is harmful when a person comes into contact with it.

protest An organized, usually peaceful public demonstration where people gather to show their disapproval of something.

strike A group of workers who refuse to work until an employer agrees to meet their demands.

union An organization of workers in the same job field that bargain together for better working conditions.

Read More

Barghoorn, Linda. *Dolores Huerta: Advocate for Women and Workers*. New York: Crabtree Publishing Company, 2017.

DeVore, Brianna L. *12 Women in Equality and Social Justice*. Mankato, Minn.: Bookstaves, 2020.

Moening, Kate. *Dolores Huerta: Labor Activist*. Minneapolis: Bellwether Media, 2020.

Websites

Dolores Huerta Foundation | Dolores Huerta
https://doloreshuerta.org/dolores-huerta/

Dolores Huerta, Portrait in a Minute
https://www.youtube.com/watch?v=cxX89_ZpP2w

PBS: Dolores Huerta and the Grape Boycott
https://www.pbs.org/video/latino-americans-dolores-huerta/

Every effort has been made to ensure that these websites are appropriate for children. However, because of the nature of the Internet, it is impossible to guarantee that these sites will remain active indefinitely or that their contents will not be altered.

Index

About the Author

Gillia M. Olson is a former farm girl turned writer. She's written and edited children's books for more than 20 years. She hopes stories of great women will inspire her daughter someday, just as they have inspired her. She lives in southern Minnesota.